James Ewell Brown Stuart

Confederate General

Colonial Leaders

Lord Baltimore
English Politician and Colonist

Benjamin Banneker
American Mathematician and Astronomer

Sir William Berkeley
Governor of Virginia

William Bradford
Governor of Plymouth Colony

Jonathan Edwards
Colonial Religious Leader

Benjamin Franklin
American Statesman, Scientist, and Writer

Anne Hutchinson
Religious Leader

Cotton Mather
Author, Clergyman, and Scholar

Increase Mather
Clergyman and Scholar

James Oglethorpe
Humanitarian and Soldier

William Penn
Founder of Democracy

Sir Walter Raleigh
English Explorer and Author

Caesar Rodney
American Patriot

John Smith
English Explorer and Colonist

Miles Standish
Plymouth Colony Leader

Peter Stuyvesant
Dutch Military Leader

George Whitefield
Clergyman and Scholar

Roger Williams
Founder of Rhode Island

John Winthrop
Politician and Statesman

John Peter Zenger
Free Press Advocate

Revolutionary War Leaders

John Adams
Second U.S. President

Samuel Adams
Patriot

Ethan Allen
Revolutionary Hero

Benedict Arnold
Traitor to the Cause

John Burgoyne
British General

George Rogers Clark
American General

Lord Cornwallis
British General

Thomas Gage
British General

King George III
English Monarch

Nathanael Greene
Military Leader

Nathan Hale
Revolutionary Hero

Alexander Hamilton
First U.S. Secretary of the Treasury

John Hancock
President of the Continental Congress

Patrick Henry
American Statesman and Speaker

William Howe
British General

John Jay
First Chief Justice of the Supreme Court

Thomas Jefferson
Author of the Declaration of Independence

John Paul Jones
Father of the U.S. Navy

Thaddeus Kosciuszko
Polish General and Patriot

Lafayette
French Freedom Fighter

James Madison
Father of the Constitution

Francis Marion
The Swamp Fox

James Monroe
American Statesman

Thomas Paine
Political Writer

Molly Pitcher
Heroine

Paul Revere
American Patriot

Betsy Ross
American Patriot

Baron Von Steuben
American General

George Washington
First U.S. President

Anthony Wayne
American General

Famous Figures of the Civil War Era

John Brown
Abolitionist

Jefferson Davis
Confederate President

Frederick Douglass
Abolitionist and Author

Stephen A. Douglas
Champion of the Union

David Farragut
Union Admiral

Ulysses S. Grant
Military Leader and President

Stonewall Jackson
Confederate General

Joseph E. Johnston
Confederate General

Robert E. Lee
Confederate General

Abraham Lincoln
Civil War President

George Gordon Meade
Union General

George McClellan
Union General

William Henry Seward
Senator and Statesman

Philip Sheridan
Union General

William Sherman
Union General

Edwin Stanton
Secretary of War

Harriet Beecher Stowe
Author of Uncle Tom's Cabin

James Ewell Brown Stuart
Confederate General

Sojourner Truth
Abolitionist, Suffragist, and Preacher

Harriet Tubman
Leader of the Underground Railroad

Famous Figures of the Civil War Era

James Ewell Brown Stuart

Confederate General

Meg Greene

Arthur M. Schlesinger, jr.
Senior Consulting Editor

Chelsea House Publishers

Philadelphia

CHELSEA HOUSE PUBLISHERS
Editor-in-Chief Sally Cheney
Director of Production Kim Shinners
Production Manager Pamela Loos
Art Director Sara Davis
Production Editor Diann Grasse

Staff for *JAMES EWELL BROWN STUART*
Editor Sally Cheney
Associate Art Director Takeshi Takahashi
Series Design Keith Trego
Layout by D&G Limited, LLC

The Chelsea House World Wide Web address is
http://www.chelseahouse.com

First Printing
1 3 5 7 9 8 6 4 2

Library of Congress Cataloging-in-Publication Data

Greene, Meg.
    Jeb Stuart : Confederate general / Meg Greene.
        p. cm. — (Famous figures of the Civil War era)
    Includes bibliographical references and index.
    ISBN 0-7910-6414-X (alk. paper) — ISBN 0-7910-6415-8 (pbk. : alk. paper)
      1. Stuart, Jeb, 1833-1864—Juvenile literature.
    2. Generals—Confederate States of America—
    Biography—Juvenile literature. 3. Confederate States of America. Army—Biography—Juvenile literature.
    4. United States—History—Civil War, 1861-1865—Calvary operations—Juvenile literature. [1. Stuart, Jeb, 1833-1864—Juvenile literature. 2. Generals. 3. United States—History—Civil War, 1861-1865.] I. Title.
    II. Series.

    E467.1.S9 G74 2001
    973.7'3'092—dc21
    [B]   2001028768

Contents

Men, women, and children were taken from Africa and brought to the United States. They were then sold to plantation owners in the South. Slaves worked for little or no money in the fields and homes of their owners, and they had no rights or freedoms. This arrangement benefited the plantation owners and was an important part of the Southern economy.

Young James

Among the finest cavalry officers on either side of the Civil War was James Ewell Brown, or "Jeb," Stuart as he later came to be called. Stuart was one of the great and most colorful figures of the Civil War, and one of the most celebrated generals in American military history.

At eleven thirty on the morning of February 6, 1833, the Stuarts of Patrick County, Virginia, welcomed the newest member of their family. James Ewell Brown Stuart, known alternately as James, Jim, or Jimmy, was the seventh child and youngest son of

Archibald and Elizabeth Stuart. In time, the family grew to include 10 children, 4 boys and 6 girls.

The Stuart family was among the most prominent in Virginia. Both sides of the family claimed ancestors who had distinguished themselves in the Revolutionary War. In addition to military officers, the family included judges and representatives to both the Virginia State Assembly and the United States House of Representatives. In fact, Archibald Stuart enjoyed a considerable reputation as a politician and lawyer. He had a great talent for public speaking, but demonstrated less ability as a businessman. Although never prospering, he was not poor and managed always to provide for his family. Archibald's political and legal responsibilities kept him away from home for long periods of time, leaving his wife to look after the daily operation of the farm and the upbringing of the children.

James spent his childhood at the family farm called Laurel Hill, located in Patrick County near the border between Virginia and North Carolina.

The southwestern part of Virginia, in the foothills of the Blue Ridge Mountains, was known as the Piedmont. The land was marked by rugged hills and forests.

Laurel Hill was not a large plantation. It was, rather, a farm on which Archibald Stuart grew tobacco and corn and raised livestock. Like larger **plantations**, however, Laurel Hill was home to a community of slaves. Around the time of James's birth in 1833, the Stuart household consisted of 12 whites and 19 blacks. By 1840, a total of 40 people called Laurel Hill home: 12 whites and 28 blacks, of which 11 were less than 10 years old.

As a child James never remembered being bored. If he was not playing with his brothers and sisters, he was doing his chores or learning from his mother how to read and write. One of his favorite activities was roaming the countryside, for James had developed an abiding love of nature. He also learned to ride at an early age, and in a short time proved to be an excellent horseman.

James was a sensitive boy, often displaying great compassion. As a child he enjoyed writing poetry, often dedicating his verses to nature and his horses. At the same time, James was not above enjoying a good joke, and, when necessary, he knew how to take care of himself in the presence of his more rough-and-tumble brothers and cousins. Courage and honor became important to James at an early age.

In 1845 two events marked a turning point in James's life. First, like his older brothers, James promised his mother that he would never touch a drop of liquor. Disapproving of her husband's fond-

When James was about nine years old, he and his brother spotted a hornet's nest in the branches of a large tree. The boys threw short sticks at the nest to knock it down. Then they climbed the tree, carrying longer sticks so they could push the nest out of the branches. Suddenly, the hornets attacked them. James's brother was stung several times, and he climbed down from the tree. James, however, closed his eyes and continued to strike at the nest, at last bringing it down. Although covered with painful stings, James had prevailed. He was willing to take risks and pay the price to prove himself and to succeed.

ness for drink, Mrs. Stuart made her sons vow never to drink alcoholic beverages. Second, James's mother decided to send him away to school. By the time James left home to make his way in the world he was well aware of his family history. He swore to himself that he, too, would one day exalt the family name. Yet, if he were to succeed, he would have to do it on his own merits. A good and respected name would carry him only so far.

During the next three years, James attended a number of different schools in Wytheville, Virginia, where he studied mathematics, Latin, spelling, and history. These "schools" were usually nothing more than a small group of children gathered in the room of a private home, receiving lessons from a local **tutor**. Because Wytheville was a good distance from his home, James boarded with various relatives or family friends, and on occasion lived in the house of his schoolmaster. In his letters to his family, James described his life. Once he explained how he had managed to avoid fighting; in another letter he described seeing a beautiful colt. He also wrote of his studies. In a letter from January 1847, he stated that he was "jogging away at old Caesar." In a letter from April of the same year he lamented his difficulty understanding algebra. Not long after he had written this letter, James fell ill with the mumps and had to spend several months under a doctor's care. A sign of his maturity came when, upon recovering from his illness, James insisted on paying the doctor's bill himself.

While a student in Wytheville, James worked in a lawyer's office to get a better sense of his father's profession. For a time, he considered becoming a schoolteacher. But James found that he had higher ambitions that teaching school could not fulfill.

In 1848, James finished his basic schooling and entered the Methodist college, Emory & Henry, located near Abingdon, Virginia. Emory & Henry had been established only 10 years earlier and was the first college located in

J.E.B. Stuart faced a personal turning point at the same time that the country was facing a time of change. In 1845, James K. Polk, portrayed above was starting his term as president and Congress had just voted to annex Texas into the United States.

southwestern Virginia. During his first year at college, a Methodist Revival meeting came to campus. James attended, and the experience was so intense that he converted to Methodism, and remained devoutly religious throughout his life.

At college, James studied engineering, history, and the classics, and joined a literary and debating society. During one debate, James became so absorbed in his topic that he lost his balance and fell off the stage.

James also engaged in extracurricular activities of which the college administration did not approve. He got into numerous fights. Once James got into a scuffle with another classmate right before he was to take a history test. His opponent bloodied James's nose, and taking care of his injury cost him 30 minutes of the exam time, forcing him to rush through the questions. Despite his antics, James graduated from Emory & Henry in 1850.

As with many new college graduates, the question arose about what to do next? Because he would not inherit enough land or wealth to support himself, James needed a career. Before choosing a profession, James decided that he needed additional training and education. One of the best and most **prestigious** schools in the country was the United States Military Academy in West Point, New York. Fortunately for James, his father knew the delegate to the United States House of Representatives from their district, who secured James an appointment to West Point. In April when James departed for West Point he did not yet realize that he had just embarked on a brief, tumultuous, and yet brilliant military career.

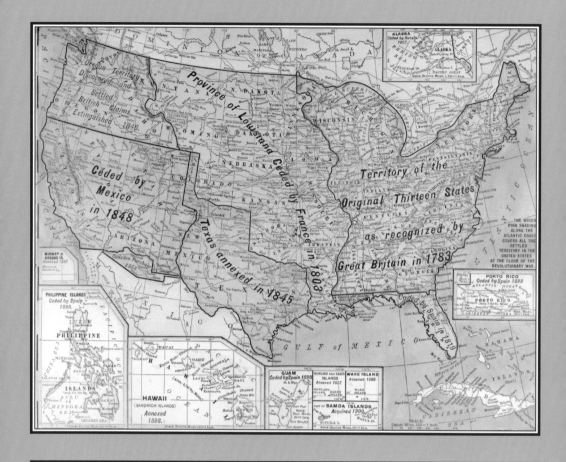

Many Americans believed in "Manifest Destiny." This was the concept that the United States was destined to reach from the Atlantic to the Pacific Ocean. This map shows how the United States looked in the 1800s. As the country grew, the question of whether or not new states would be free states, or allow slavery, became important.

2

West Point Cadet Stuart

On July 1, 1850, "**Cadet**" Stuart officially entered West Point. By this time, the 17-year-old James had grown into a plain looking young man, standing about 5' 10" tall, with long arms and legs. He had a high forehead and a full face, and although his nose was prominent, it was his blue-gray eyes that caught people's attention. In time, James grew a moustache and full beard, but kept his brown hair clipped and neat.

Early on during his West Point career, James received a new nickname, "Beauty." The name, as one classmate later explained, was a joke. James's appearance was the exact opposite. James never shed his nickname. Even after he achieved the rank of major general, his classmates could still be heard to address him as "Dear Beauty."

Within two weeks of his arrival at West Point, James wrote home complaining that he had not received any letters from family members. He also promised in a letter to his father that he would write home every two weeks, and that he would **diligently apply** himself to his studies. "I know that if I *try* I can go through," he wrote, "and I am determined to *try*." This initial homesickness soon passed, and James plunged into life at West Point.

Three times a day he and other new cadets, known as "plebes," drilled in infantry tactics. Like the other new recruits, James was also subject to the merciless teasing and pranks by the upperclassmen, which was a tradition of cadet life. James also maintained his reputation for fighting as he continued to accept every challenge, whether it came from a plebe or an upperclassman.

When James was not fighting, he was busy with his classes. During his time at West Point, James concentrated on courses in mathematics, philosophy, history, chemistry, English, rhetoric (speaking), French, and drawing. He was also required to attend classes on cavalry tactics and riding, where he soon established a reputation as one of the finest horsemen at the academy. In describing his riding drills, James often poked fun at the "ridiculous figures [the] Yankees cut on horseback."

James learned that his "free" education, courtesy of the United States government, was not really free. During their stay at West Point, cadets received $24 a month from the government, a generous sum for the times. The money was put directly into an account at the academy commissary and was used to pay for clothing, uniforms, and personal items. Unfortunately, James, like many of his classmates, found that the monthly allowance was never enough to cover his expenses. As he was not receiving financial help from his family, James was always in debt to the commissary.

James was generally enthusiastic about his studies. He wrote, "I know of no profession more desirable than that of the soldier. Indeed every thing connected with the Academy has far **surpassed** my … expectations." From the band to the many military ceremonies and parades, James loved it all.

He excelled at the experience of military training and particularly liked the way in which cadets were graded at West Point. In every class, each student was ranked based on their performance in the classroom. At the end of every semester, the rankings were posted for all to see. For James, it offered an opportunity to measure himself against his peers. If it meant he had to study harder, then he was willing to do so. Learning now had become a sort of competition in which James wanted to participate, as he admitted in his correspondence:

> I used to think that I had some idea of what hard study was, at least my idea of it was that it was something to be avoided as much as possible which before I came here I succeeded at admirably, but on coming here I found that it was necessary to cultivate a more intimate acquaintance with it or else come out wanting at the Examination. So I turned into studying pretty hard.

During his time at West Point, he showed a slow and steady improvement in his courses. Compared to some of the other cadets who had benefited from a superior educational background, James was not as well prepared in some areas. He struggled in English class, for example, but eventually mastered the basic rules of grammar.

Probably the toughest class for most cadets was mathematics, and those who failed had to leave the academy. Luckily, James had a natural aptitude for math. At the end of his first year, therefore, his grades were good enough to rank him eighth out of his class of 72.

Despite his love of a good fight, James made many friends at West Point. During this time of mounting tension between the North and the South, James also became more aware of his identity as a Virginian and as a Southerner. He had little use for the "Yankees" (Northerners) at the academy, often making fun of the way they talked and acted. He mostly sought the

The tension between the North and the South that James felt at West Point would escalate in a few years into Civil War. Jefferson Davis would be the president of the Confederate States of America, which was made up of the proslavery Southern states.

company of other cadets from Virginia and the South.

By his second year at the academy, James had earned the rank of corporal of the corps, the third highest rank available to second-year students. While he took his responsibilities seriously, he also realized that having a rank meant having special privileges.

By the time James reached his last year at the academy, he had achieved the rank of second captain of the corps. He was also one of eight cadets chosen for the position of "cavalry officer" in recognition of their superior horsemanship. James spent many hours with his horse, Don Quixote, practicing with his **saber** as he charged a row of dummy heads placed on posts in the academy riding hall. James also kept busy with his studies in mineralogy, geology, and engineering, in addition to courses in infantry, artillery, and cavalry tactics. When James graduated from West Point in 1854, he ranked 13th in a class of 46 cadets.

Still, the 18-year-old James was at a loss about what to do with his life. Writing to his father, he described this *"important crisis* of my life." As a West Point graduate, James owed the United States government eight years of military service. At this time, though, there were not nearly enough positions in the army to accommodate all West Point graduates. Because of this imbalance, the army allowed graduates to return immediately to civilian life.

As James saw it, he had two choices: he could either pursue a career in the military, which promised **"ample** support with a life of hardship and uncertainty," or he could practice law, which to James seemed "an overcrowded thoroughfare which may or may not yield a support." James did not want his father's advice. He instead believed that God would provide him with the answers he sought.

Finally, James made his decision. He had grown accustomed to military life during his time at West Point, and he generally liked it. In a letter he wrote shortly after graduation, he stated that "the taste of classmates for each other's society particularly West Pointers is unequalled ... and what is more remarkable it becomes more and more intense as time continues. A thought which makes me fear that *out of the army* I will be miserably unhappy." James Stuart was going to be a soldier. By the summer of 1854 James was back in Virginia, awaiting his orders from the War Department.

James was assigned to a cavalry unit in the frontier of Texas and then was sent to St. Louis. Native Americans rode on horseback and attacked settlers in an effort to protect their families and land.

Frontier Soldier

During the summer of 1854, Lieutenant James Stuart received his orders. On October 15, he was to present himself to the commanding officer of the Mounted Rifles, a cavalry unit, at Fort McIntosh in Laredo, Texas, a post situated in the southern part of the state. James's first reaction was disappointment, for he had hoped to be assigned to the more prestigious post at Jefferson Barracks in St. Louis, Missouri.

After battling a terrible bout of seasickness during the boat trip from New Orleans to Galveston, Texas, James finally arrived at his new home in October.

Eager to begin fighting Native Americans, James was in for another disappointment. Writing to a cousin a year later, he described life at the fort: "Notwithstanding we have threaded every trail, clambered every precipice and penetrated every ravine for hundreds of miles around, we have not been able to find Mr. Comanche. We are now quietly awaiting General Smith's orders, resting our animals."

James complained that the soldiers had to do so much walking over the rocky **terrain**, that he had completely worn out his pair of heavy soled boots and would have gone barefooted except for a pair of embroidered slippers he had thought to bring with him to Texas.

Despite the lack of action, James found much to like about his new home. The hunting was plentiful; James saw animals he had never seen before, such as antelope, blue quail, and Chapparal Cocks. He was particularly fascinated with prairie dogs, and he spent hours watching them in the desert. When he was not hunting or riding about the prairie, James was busy writing letters to family and to a newspaper in Staunton, Virginia, *The Jeffersonian*, describing his adventures on the Texas frontier. It was in Texas, too, that James decided to grow his famous mustache and beard. One of James's friends said that James was "the only man he ever saw that [a] beard improved."

In the spring of 1855, James learned that he was to report to Jefferson Barracks in St. Louis as second lieutenant of the newly formed 1st Cavalry, one of two new units created by Secretary of War, Jefferson Davis. Davis believed that large and swift cavalry forces could better endure long **campaigns** against the Native Americans.

That May, James left Texas to join his new unit in St. Louis. Once there, he was appointed regimental quartermaster, or the officer in charge of the supplies and equipment. Although James had hoped for a better duty, he again made the most of his time, learning invaluable lessons about how to care for large groups of horses.

James rode with Colonel Edwin Sumner's cavalry, which was called to Kansas to keep peace between free-soil and proslavery forces.

By the summer, James was on the move once more. This time his destination was Fort Leavenworth in the Kansas territory. It was here that James met and fell in love with Flora Cooke, the daughter of Colonel Philip St. George Cooke of the 2nd Dragoons. Flora descended from one of the prominent families in Virginia. She had been educated at private schools and was, among other things, an accomplished rider. Flora totally captivated James, and he was soon writing her love letters. She did nothing to discourage his affections. On November 14, 1855, the couple married and set up housekeeping in the officers' quarters at Fort Leavenworth.

In the midst of James's happiness, trouble was brewing in Kansas. In 1854 Congress had passed the Kansas-Nebraska Act after months of bitter debate. The bill allowed for the residents of Kansas and Nebraska, rather than Congress, to decide for themselves whether to allow slavery in their territories. As a result, streams of proslavery and antislavery settlers, known as "free soilers," flooded the region in an attempt to settle the slavery question. Whichever side could get the most voters to the polls could determine whether Kansas would be a slave territory or free.

It became clear early on that there was little hope of finding a peaceful resolution to the argument. Beginning in 1854 and continuing for the next five years, the Kansas territory was torn by a series of border wars. Both sides engaged in horse stealing, arson, destruction of property, lynching, and murder. In time, the area became known as "Bleeding Kansas."

James and the 1st Cavalry were often called upon to maintain law and order between the warring settlers. On June 5, 1856, James rode with a detachment of men under the command of Colonel Edwin Sumner into a camp of free-soilers led by abolitionist John Brown. Just three days earlier, Brown and a band of his followers, which included his sons, had attacked a group of militia and captured some of the soldiers. Sumner ordered Brown to free his prisoners and to disband the group.

While the army acted as peacekeeper among the settlers, members of the Cheyenne nation were also causing problems in Kansas, raiding and killing settlers along the trails that passed through the territory. Because these actions

"The Tragic Prelude," a mural by John Steuart Curry, hangs in the Topeka, Kansas, State Capitol. It depicts John Brown's life-long fight against slavery.

violated earlier treaties, the U.S. government ordered the 1st Cavalry to begin a campaign against the Native Americans. In carrying out this assignment, James received his first command when he was placed in charged of G Company.

In the May 1857, James left Fort Leavenworth in pursuit of the Cheyenne. The four cavalry companies were accompanied by 300 cattle for food and 50 wagons carrying provisions and supplies. The group traveled for almost two months, stopping at Fort Kearny to add reinforcements before heading for Fort Laramie. After almost 18 months on the frontier, James at last took part in combat.

On July 29, 1857, the six companies encountered approximately 300 Cheyenne warriors near the Smoky Hill River in the Kansas territory. Before the Cheyenne knew what was happening, the cavalry were bearing down upon them. It was the first cavalry charge in which James had taken part, and in the process he lost track of most his company. At one point, James and three of his fellow officers were the only ones still in pursuit of the fleeing warriors.

James finally came upon his comrades who had cornered a single brave. But the brave had a revolver and was about to shoot one of James's friends. James charged the enemy with his saber drawn. The brave fired at James, but missed. Another soldier yelled, "Wait! I'll fetch him." As he prepared to shoot the warrior, however, his revolver accidentally discharged the last cartridge he had. The soldier was defenseless. James charged again. As he swung his sword down toward the brave, he heard a shot. The muzzle of the Native American's gun was only a foot away from James when he fired, and the blast hit James in the chest.

Miraculously, the bullet struck James's breast-bone, and instead of shattering it, bounced off and lodged in the soft tissue on the left side of his chest. James was already down by the time his comrades killed the attacker. James was not seriously wounded. He was stiff and in pain for weeks after the incident, but he fully recovered.

James returned to Fort Leavenworth in August, just in time for the birth of his first child, a

During the winter of 1858-1859, James worked on two inventions specifically designed for cavalrymen. The first was the "Stuart's lightning horse hitcher." It consisted of a metal fixture that was attached to the leather halter of a horse. The mechanism allowed a mounted horseman to unhitch his horse more quickly, saving valuable minutes while preparing for battle.

The other invention was an attachment for cavalry saber belts, known as " a stout brass hook," which permitted a soldier to remove his sword and scabbard from his belt and attach it to a horse. The invention would make it easier for a cavalryman to dismount should he need to fight on foot. In 1859 the War Department gave James a six-month leave of absence to secure a patent for his designs and to negotiate the sale of his saber hook.

daughter, born in September. He and his wife decided to call her Flora, and James proclaimed to his friends, "I have the prettiest and smartest baby in North America." For the next year and a half, James occupied himself with his duties at the fort. During the summer of 1859, he and Flora received permission to travel to Washington, D. C., where James hoped to secure patents for two of his inventions. The trip would also give him and Flora an opportunity to visit with family and friends.

On October 17, 1859, James had come to the

offices of the War Department for an appointment. While there, he heard of a raid on the federal arsenal (a storehouse for weapons and ammunition) at Harpers Ferry, Virginia (now West Virginia). According to rumor, the attack on the arsenal was undertaken to acquire arms to carry out a slave revolt.

James volunteered to carry a message from the War Office to Colonel Robert E. Lee, then visiting family at his home in Arlington, Virginia, summoning him to take command of the troops organized to put down the uprising. James knew Lee well, having met him at West Point when Lee was superintendent of the school. He was also good friends with Lee's son, Custis, who was a cadet at West Point. Although James was considerably younger, he had become good friends with Lee, and the two had kept in contact after James's graduation.

Upon receiving orders from the War Department to return to Washington immediately, Lee asked James to serve as his **adjutant**. Together they joined 90 marines and four companies of Maryland and Virginia militia at Harpers Ferry to assess the situation. When Lee and James arrived on the scene, they learned that a handful of men, most of them white, had taken hostages and were inside the arsenal. James volunteered to take a message from Lee to the men in the hope of getting them to surrender and release the hostages unharmed. No one yet knew with whom they were dealing.

In negotiations that followed, conducted through the slightly opened door of the arsenal, it was James who recognized the leader of the group as John Brown, the abolitionist from Kansas. Refusing to give in to Brown's demands, James turned to leave. In doing so, he waved his hat, a signal to the marines and the militia that talks had broken off. They were now to charge the building. It was all over in a matter of minutes. The soldiers stormed the armory and freed all the hostages without injury. They took Brown and two other of his followers into custody, but

Robert E. Lee was a skilled military leader in the U.S. Army before he joined the South as a general in the Civil War. In 1859 James and Lee fought together at Harpers Ferry against Abolitionist John Brown.

killed the rest of his group, including Brown's sons, in the skirmish.

By December 1859, James was back in Kansas, again in pursuit of renegade Native Americans. While he had witnessed two of the most important events in American history, "Bleeding Kansas" and John Brown's raid at Harpers Ferry, James, like many Americans, did not fully realize the depth of the growing division between the North and the South. By 1860 the crisis had grown so heated that Southerners threatened to **secede**, or break away from, the United States and form their own nation. With the election of Abraham Lincoln as president in November 1860, Southerners made their decision. On December 20, 1860, South Carolina became the first state to secede from the union.

By this time, James was seeking a promotion to captain. As he waited to hear whether he would receive his new rank, several more Southern states left the Union, and the newly formed Confederate army had fired upon the federal army stationed inside Fort Sumter in the harbor off the coast of Charleston, South Carolina.

Learning in April 1860 that he would receive his promotion, James also learned that Virginia had seceded from the Union. James quickly decided what to do. Suddenly, his long-anticipated promotion seemed to pale in comparison to events taking place on the national stage. "I go with Virginia," he declared.

Fort Sumter was a Union outpost in Charleston Harbor, off the coast of South Carolina. The fort was attacked by Confederate forces on April 12, 1861. This attack marked the start of the Civil War.

In 1861, Colonel Thomas "Stonewall" Jackson put James in charge of a cavalry regiment in the Confederate army. Jackson later became a general. In 1863 he was accidentally shot by his own men at the Battle of Chancellorsville and died from his wounds.

"The Eyes of the Army"

On May 10, 1861, only a week after he had resigned his commission in the United States Army, James reported for duty to Colonel Thomas J. "Stonewall" Jackson at Harpers Ferry, Virginia. At first, Jackson did not know what to do with his new charge. James's commission was in the infantry, but Jackson wanted to place James in charge of all Virginia cavalry companies. To do so, however, was to risk offending a senior officer, Captain Turner Ashby. In the end, Jackson decided to split the cavalry companies, giving each man a regiment, which was made up of approximately 350 men. When

General Joseph E. Johnston arrived to take command of the Army of Northern Virginia, James, now a lieutenant colonel in the army of the Confederate States of America, remained in charge of his regiment.

James and his men did not have to wait long to see action. Union troops were already advancing into Virginia. General Johnston, not yet ready to engage them, pulled back toward Winchester, Virginia, approximately 25 miles southwest of Harpers Ferry. So Johnston could prepare his troops for combat, he gave James the dangerous mission of controlling an area more than 50 miles long to screen enemy troop movements and deflect Union fire. This mission enabled Johnston to organize his forces for a march on Manassas Junction (Bull Run) in Northern Virginia.

James soon emerged as the master of modern cavalry tactics. He reasoned that more accurate long-range rifles and artillery had rendered old-style cavalry charges obsolete. To be useful,

The first major battle of the Civil War took place near Manassas Junction on the Bull Run River. James and his cavalry contributed to the Confederate victory at the First Battle of Bull Run (also called Manassas).

therefore, the cavalry had to take a different approach to combat and to fill a different role in the army.

James also realized that to be effective the cavalry must dominate the ground in between opposing armies. Unlike the Union horsemen who rode in smaller units scattered throughout the entire army, James believed that a large, unified cavalry would provide tremendous advantages. A large cavalry could be used to raid, wreck, and disrupt the enemy's lines of supply and communication. The most important strategic cavalry operation was scouting and **reconnaissance**, or gathering information about terrain as well as enemy strength and troop movements. This **intelligence** helped commanders make better decisions on how, when, and where to attack. In this respect, the commander of a cavalry could select the ground on which a battle would be fought, and thus could put his army at a great advantage.

Throughout the war, every opportunity to engage Union troops taught James a lesson in strategy and tactics. On one occasion, he led his men directly into enemy lines, where he almost got them deliberately surrounded by the enemy. He later explained that there might come a time when they found themselves in precisely that situation, and they needed to know how to fight their way out. On the advance toward Manassas, James and his men had unexpectedly run into a company of Union troops. Although severely outnumbered, James marched his men toward the enemy, ordering them to dismount and fight on foot. After a brief skirmish, James commanded his men to withdraw by marching backward and firing their guns. When the men reached their horses, they mounted and prepared to gallop away. But James ordered them to bring their horses to a trot and not allow them to gallop.

When they had reached safety, James explained to his men:

> You are brave fellows, and patriotic ones too, but you are ignorant of this kind of work, and I am teaching you. I want you to observe that a good man on a good horse can never be caught. Another thing: cavalry can trot away from anything and a gallop is a gait unbecoming a soldier, unless he is going toward the enemy. Remember that. We gallop toward the enemy, and trot away, always.

Confederate soldiers are shown resting at their camp between battles. James's well-trained cavalry set an example for other soldiers and added to the confidence of the Confederate army.

As he finished speaking, James told his men, "Steady now! don't break ranks!" The men then heard an explosion and the hissing of a shell flying over their heads. "There," said James, "I've been waiting for that, and watching those fellows. I knew they'd shoot too high, and I wanted you to learn how shells sound." James's methods may have been unusual, but there is no doubt that his men were confident and skilled. They must have wondered, though, whether they were attending school or fighting a war.

By July, James and his troops had rejoined the main Confederate army converging on Manassas Junction. At the First Battle of Bull Run (also called Manassas), which took place between July 16 and July 22, 1861, James and his cavalry proved invaluable to Johnston. The **intelligence** they provided about the deployment of enemy troops helped Johnston to direct artillery fire against the Union lines and led General Jubal Early and his men to a key position on the battlefield that forced a Union retreat. As the first major battle of the Civil War, Manassas was an important victory for the Confederates. Johnston thought James's contribution so essential to the success of his army that, two years later upon learning that he was to take command of the Army of Tennessee, Johnston wrote to James: "How can I eat, sleep, or rest in peace without you at the outpost?"

As a result of his actions during the first few months of the war, James earned a promotion to brigadier general on September 24, 1861. He now commanded the cavalry units attached to the main eastern army of the Confederacy, which would soon be commanded by General Robert E. Lee. James's new techniques for utilizing the cavalry continued to give an important advantage to the Confederate army during the early years of the war and gained him a reputation that went beyond the campfires and tents of his men. Because of his unusual training style, his men also quickly rode and acted like battle-seasoned veterans, adding to the confidence and enthusiasm of the Confederate troops.

In June 1862, James became even more famous. Union General George B. McClellan

Shown here is Richmond, Virginia, which was the capital of the Confederacy.

was preparing to move several thousand Federal troops toward Richmond, Virginia, the capital of the Confederacy. General Lee decided that the best way to stop McClellan and his army would be to attack on the Union right flank, or side, and to the rear. To observe the movement of the Union forces, Lee ordered James and his cavalry to keep a close watch on them.

In the early morning hours of June 12, 1862, James's staff was awakened with the words, "Gentlemen, in ten minutes every man must be in his saddle!" James's appearance made for an inspiring sight. "As he mounted his horse on that moonlit night he was a gallant figure to look at," remembered one member of his command. Dressed in a gray coat, with a saber and pistol at his side, James also sported the tall black boots of the cavalry, which came to just above the knee, and a brown hat with a black plume that appeared to float in the air. Asked when he and his men would return, James laughed and replied, "It may be for years, and it may be forever."

For the next three days, James led 1,200 men on a 100-mile ride behind Union lines to gather the information Lee needed to plan his attack. The Confederates managed to destroy enemy property, including a Union supply train of 200 wagons, and to steal 300 horses and mules and capture 170 prisoners, with 4 Union officers among that number.

Union forces tried repeatedly to capture the elusive Confederate cavalrymen without success. James not only reported back to General Lee in a timely fashion, but completed his mission with only one casualty. To the delight of many, he caused great embarrassment to the Union army. In fact, it was said that President Lincoln decided to replace McClellan as commander of the Union Army of the Potomac in part as the result of McClellan's apparent helplessness to stop James. From that point on, Lee considered James to be the eyes of the army, so great were his skills at obtaining information.

President Lincoln (standing, center) meeting with Union General George McClellan (facing him) on the battle-field. Lincoln was displeased by McClellan's failure to reach Richmond.

Sometime after James had completed his celebrated ride around Union forces, he was talking to General James Longstreet. James told his friend Longstreet, "I left one general behind me." When Longstreet asked James the name of the general, James joked, "General Consternation." While James would never admit it, he was having the time of his life. As a result of his daring ride around McClellan, James became a hero throughout the Confederacy. More than that, he earned a new nickname. From now on he was known not as James, Jimmy, or "Beauty." He was now, and forever, "Jeb" Stuart.

One of James's greatest regrets during his ride around McClellan's forces was not meeting his father-in-law, who had decided to support the Union cause and was with the Army of the Potomac. James was so angry at Philip St. George Cooke's decision that he and Flora renamed their second child. The boy was originally named after his mother's father, his maternal grandfather. James and Flora had considered a number of other possibilities, but finally decided on J.E.B. Stuart Jr., known ever after as Jimmy.

The Confederate army was victorious at the Battle
of Chancelorsville because of Jeb Stuart's skills at
information gathering and leading his men during
battle.

"The Greatest Cavalryman in America"

By the summer of 1862, Jeb Stuart had established himself as one of the greatest heroes of the Confederacy. Thanks to a recent promotion in July, Jeb now held the rank of major general and was in charge of an entire cavalry division. Not only that, but poems, songs, stories, and legends celebrated his dashing appearance, from his plumed hat to his golden spurs. As Stuart swept from victory to victory, his soldiers came to think of him as a military genius.

In reality, Jeb worked very hard and was careful in collecting information, and his successful missions were often the product of spies who had earlier gone out to scout the terrain and chart enemy troop movements. In this way, Jeb knew ahead of time what he and his men were likely to face. Jeb also made sure that he employed the best and most reliable men as spies, often using soldiers who were already familiar with the territory.

After his amazing ride around General McClellan's forces, Jeb went on to play an important role in several other Confederate victories. Riding with the Army of Northern Virginia, Jeb led a raid against Catlett's Station on August 22, 1862, during which, among other things, he stole Union General John Pope's uniform and dispatch book, which contained important military correspondence, in addition to money chests that contained $500,000 in cash and another $20,000 in gold. The following October, Jeb and his men took 1,200 horses during a raid in Chambersburg,

Pennsylvania. Each new exploit brought new glory and praise for Jeb. It seemed as if he had achieved the fame and recognition he always sought.

In the spring of 1863, Jeb and his cavalry again distinguished themselves during the battle of Chancellorsville. During a reconnaissance mission, Jeb discovered that one side of General Joseph Hooker's Union force was completely exposed and thus vulnerable to attack. He relayed the information to Confederate General "Stonewall" Jackson, who then marched his men to mount an assault on Hooker's flank. On the night of May 2, 1863, however, General Jackson was mortally wounded by soldiers from his own 18th North Carolina regiment who, in the dark, mistook him for a Union officer. Jackson had his left arm amputated, but died eight days later. Soon thereafter, Jeb received word that he was now in command of Jackson's infantry corps. Jeb carried out the difficult task of reconnecting with Lee's troops, while at the same time pounding Hooker's troops with Confederate artillery. While the Confederate Army scored another important victory at Chancellorsville, with Jeb playing an important part in it, the accomplishment had come at a high cost.

But Jeb's run of good luck was nearing its end. In June 1863, the victorious Confederate Army of Northern Virginia streamed into Culpeper County, Virginia. The Confederates had won the Second Battle of Bull Run (Manassas) and now seemed invincible as they prepared to invade Pennsylvania to bring the war to the North. But victory was taking its toll: Lee's men were half-starved, and much of their equipment was lost or falling apart. The men were also weak after defeating armies twice their size at Chancellorsville and Manassas. But Lee was determined to strike the North not only to capture horses, equipment, weapons, supplies, and food for his men, but also to

The Confederate army won the Second Battle of Bull Run (Manassas) and prepared to invade Pennsylvania in an attempt to lead the war into the North.

win that one decisive victory that would end the war.

By June 5, 1863, two infantry corps under Generals Longstreet and Ewell were encamped at Culpeper. Six miles north of town, holding the line of the Rappahannock River, Jeb had stationed his men to screen the Confederate army against a surprise attack. On June 9, however, under cover of dense fog, 10,000 Union horsemen massed on the other side. Misinterpreting the screening action of Jeb's cavalry, Union General Alfred Pleasanton thought he was attacking an enemy raiding party of unknown strength.

Early that morning, Jeb heard ragged gunfire coming from the direction of the river. Soon Confederate troopers reached his headquarters with the news that Union cavalrymen were coming up a narrow road near the camp. Just as Jeb heard that the enemy had been checked at St. James, he received the startling information that Union troops were riding in from the rear. Only a lone artillery piece was at Jeb's camp, as well as a small group of men to guard the headquarters. Jeb ordered the single gun fired; the Union horsemen halted their advance. Racing against time, the rest of the Confederate cavalry rushed back to meet this new threat.

Never before had the Union cavalry shown such strength and skill in combat. Jeb's headquarters was overrun, and the rear lines of the Confederate army were threatened. Another cavalry unit rode in, saving Jeb and his men. After 12 hours of battle, Union troops retreated to the north side of the river. At the Battle of Brandy Station more than 19,000 men participated in the largest cavalry battle ever to take place in the Western Hemisphere. For the first time in the Civil War, Union cavalry matched the Confederate horsemen in skill and determination.

Lee was nevertheless determined to press on to Pennsylvania. In late June, Jeb received orders to screen Lee's advance, but he decided instead to engage in another ride around Union forces and begin his own march north keeping to the east of the Union army.

Jeb's decision to strike out on his own proved to be a terrible mistake. On his journey north, he captured 150 supply wagons, which although badly needed by the Confederates, slowed Jeb and his men down considerably, and made it more difficult to carry out his most important duty, which was scouting for Lee's army. By the time General Lee and the Army of Northern Virginia had gathered in Gettysburg,

The Confederates lost the decisive Battle of Gettysburg in Pennsylvania. The fighting lasted from July 1 to July 3, 1863.

Pennsylvania, at the end of June, Jeb was nowhere to be found. Lee had had to move blindly over unfamiliar country, and did not yet know for certain the location of Union forces.

In the end, Jeb's actions cost Lee valuable time and robbed him of vital information that he needed at the Battle of Gettysburg. Legend has it that when Jeb finally arrived on July 2 at General Lee's headquarters, Lee greeted him by saying, "Well, General Stuart, you are here at last," and nothing more. While Jeb led a valiant charge against Union forces on July 3, his efforts failed. In an attempt to cover up his errors, Jeb tried to excel on the battlefield.

For the next year, Jeb continued to fight for Confederate independence. It was becoming evident, though, that the tide was turning toward the North. Increasingly, Jeb's and other Confederate units were outnumbered and outgunned by the enemy. Moreover, the Union cavalrymen had learned from their defeats and were now showing themselves to be the equals of the Confederates.

On May 11, 1864, Jeb was thrown into an encounter with Union General Philip Sheridan. Sheridan was on his way to Richmond with plans to lure Jeb's troop away from the main Confederate force and destroy it. The two forces met at Yellow Tavern, six miles north of Richmond. At one point during the battle, Union troops made a mounted charge. Yelling, "Give it to them, boys!", Jeb waved his sword and rode toward the oncoming enemy. He fired his pistol at enemy soldiers, as other Confederates on horseback galloped past him.

Suddenly one Union soldier on the ground fired his pistol at Jeb. A .44 caliber bullet struck Jeb's right side, just below his ribs, giving him the second wound of his military career. Somehow, Jeb stayed in the saddle, as he clasped his side. Quickly his men gathered around him,

Jeb Stuart's men fought with Union General Philip Sheridan's troop at Yellow Tavern, six miles north of Richmond, Virginia. Jeb was mortally wounded in the battle.

calling for a doctor, while trying to lead Jeb away from the fighting. Soon an ambulance wagon arrived and Jeb was loaded into it. Seeing some of the Confederate soldiers leaving the field, Jeb called out to them, "Go back! go back! and do your duty, as I have done mine, and our country will be safe. Go back! Go back! I had rather die than be whipped."

Jeb was then taken to Richmond to have his wound properly tended. On the way there, one of the doctors offered him a drink of whiskey while he examined Jeb's wound. At first, Jeb refused remembering the promise he had made to his mother many years ago, but finally he agreed to take some. Looking at Jeb's wound, the doctor became very concerned. The bullet had lodged inside Jeb, and the chances were growing slim that he would survive.

A telegram was immediately sent to Flora telling her to come to Richmond at once. On the afternoon of May 12, Flora left with their two children and a military escort to go to the city and the home of a local doctor where Jeb was staying. Meanwhile, Jeb was making arrangements for the disposal of his military papers and personal effects; he knew he was going to die.

He asked that the small Confederate flag he had worn inside his hat be returned to a woman in South Carolina. He left his horses to two of his aides, while he asked that his spurs be sent to a friend in Virginia and his sword go to his son, Jeb Jr. He also asked how the fighting was going, then stated, "God grant that they be successful. But I must be prepared for another world."

That afternoon, the president of the Confederate states, Jefferson Davis, came to see Jeb. When asked how he was feeling, Jeb replied, "Easy, but willing to die, if God and my country think I have fulfilled my destiny and done my duty." Throughout the rest of the afternoon and early evening, he kept asking if Flora had arrived. At 7:38 P.M. on May 12, 1864, Jeb Stuart died at the age of 31. When Flora and the children finally did arrive in Richmond later that night, it was already too late.

At five o'clock in the afternoon on May 13, Jeb Stuart was buried in Hollywood Cemetery

In 1904 work began on a monument to honor Jeb Stuart. The Richmond City Council decided to place the statue at the intersection of Franklin and Lombardy Streets, which marked the beginning of Monument Avenue, so named for its memorials to Confederate leaders such as Robert E. Lee and Stonewall Jackson. The Stuart Monument has a plain granite stone base, which supports the figure of Stuart twisted in his saddle, facing east toward the city, and holding the reins of his galloping horse. The monument is inscribed with his name and rank as Commander of the Cavalry Corps of the Army of Northern Virginia. The City of Richmond is listed as donor of the monument. The intersection of Franklin and Lombardy Streets was renamed Stuart Circle on August 13, 1912.

in Richmond. The day was rainy and overcast; the hearse bearing Jeb's casket was topped by four black plumes, similar to those he had worn in his hat, while four white horses carried him on his final ride. At the grave, his mourners could hear the boom of cannon fire in the distance, as Confederate troops continued their fight to protect the city.

James Ewell Brown Stuart was among the greatest cavalry officers who ever lived. The men who fought beside him or against him recognized that he was an extraordinary soldier and leader. After Jeb's death, Robert E. Lee said, "I can scarcely think of him without weeping." Union commander John Sedgwick, who had fought against Jeb, called him "the greatest cavalryman ... in America." In his final hours, Jeb gave away his horse, his sword, his spurs, and the flag under which he had fought for three years, all those things that had defined him as a soldier and a hero. To family, friends, and future generations, however, he would always be remembered as both.

GLOSSARY

adjutant-staff officer who assists the commanding officer.

ample-of large size; generous or more than adequate supply.

apply-to put into action.

cadet-a student at a military or naval academy.

campaign-a military operation.

diligently-applying honest effort to a task.

gait-the movement of a horse.

intelligence-information about the enemy.

plantations-large farms.

prestigious-well known and highly regarded.

reconnaissance-exploration to gather information.

saber-sword.

scabbard-a covering for a sword.

secede-to leave, break away.

surpassed-to go beyond the limit.

terrain-earth, land.

tutor-teacher.

CHRONOLOGY

1833   Born on February 6 in Patrick County, Virginia.

1845   Begins formal education.

1848   Enrolls at Emory & Henry College.

1850   Graduates from Emory & Henry College, begins studies at West Point.

1854   Graduates from West Point, travels to Texas for first military assignment.

1855   Meets and marries Flora Cooke, assigned to Fort Leavenworth and Riley, Kansas.

1856   Helps keep law and order during "Bleeding Kansas," where he encounters John Brown.

1857   Sees Indian action, receives first wound; daughter Flora born in September.

1859   Participates in liberation of federal arsenal at Harpers Ferry and capture of John Brown and his followers.

1861   Resigns from the U.S. Army, joins the Confederate States of America Army with the rank of colonel. Fights at the First Battle of Bull Run (Manassas); promoted to brigadier general.

1862   Rides around McClellan's forces; promoted to major general; fights at the Second Battle of Bull Run.

1863   Fights at Chancellorsville where he takes command of Jackson's troops after Jackson is mortally wounded; fights at Second Battle of Manassas and in Battle of Brandy Station; carries out disrupted mission around Union forces at Gettysburg

1864   Is mortally wounded at Yellow Tavern, Virginia, on May 11, dies on May 12 in Richmond, Virginia, and on May 13 is buried in Hollywood Cemetery in Richmond.

CIVIL WAR TIME LINE

1860   Abraham Lincoln is elected president of the United
States on November 6. During the next few months,
Southern states begin to break away from the Union.

1861   On April 12, the Confederates attack Fort Sumter,
South Carolina, and the Civil War begins. Union
forces are defeated in Virginia at the First Battle of
Bull Run (First Manassas) on July 21 and withdraw to
Washington, D.C.

1862   Robert E. Lee is placed in command of the main
Confederate army in Virginia in June. Lee defeats
the Army of the Potomac at the Second Battle of
Bull Run (Second Manassas) in Virginia on August
29–30. On September 17, Union general George B.
McClellan turns back Lee's first invasion of the
North at Antietam Creek near Sharpsburg, Maryland.
It is the bloodiest day of the war.

1863   On January 1, President Lincoln issues the Emancipation
Proclamation, freeing slaves in Southern states.
Between May 1–6, Lee wins an important victory
at Chancellorsville, but key Southern commander
Thomas J. "Stonewall" Jackson dies from wounds.
In June, Union forces hold the city of Vicksburg,
Mississippi, under siege. The people of Vicksburg
surrender on July 4. Lee's second invasion of the
North during July 1–3 is decisively turned back at
Gettysburg, Pennsylvania.

1864   General Grant is made supreme Union commander on March 9. Following a series of costly battles, on June 19 Grant successfully encircles Lee's troops in Petersburg, Virginia. A siege of the town lasts nearly a year. Union general William Sherman captures Atlanta on September 2 and begins the "March to the Sea," a campaign of destruction across Georgia and South Carolina. On November 8, Abraham Lincoln wins reelection as president.

1865   On April 2, Petersburg, Virginia, falls to the Union. Lee attempts to reach Confederate forces in North Carolina but is gradually surrounded by Union troops. Lee surrenders to Grant on April 9 at Appomattox, Virginia, ending the war. Abraham Lincoln is assassinated by John Wilkes Booth on April 14.

FURTHER READING

Blashfield, Jean F. and Wallace B. Black. *Horse Soldiers: Cavalry in the Civil War.* New York: Franklin Watts, 1998.

Corrick, James A.. *Life Among the Soldiers and Cavalry.* San Diego: Lucent Books Inc., 2000.

De Grummond Lena Y. and Lynn de Grummond Delaune. *Jeb Stuart.* Philadelphia: J. B. Lippincott Company, 1979.

Moore, Kay and Anni Matsick. *If You Lived at the Time of the Civil War.* New York: Scholastic, 1994.

Pflueger, Lynda. *Jeb Stuart: Confederate Cavalry General.* New York: Enslow Publishers, 1998.

Reger, Jamees P. *Civil War Generals of the Confederacy.* San Diego: Lucent Books Inc., 1998.

Yancey, Diane. *Leaders of the North and South: Civil War.* San Diego: Lucent Books Inc, 2000.

INDEX

Note: **Boldface** numbers indicate illustrations.

abolitionists, 32, 38
adjutant, 37–38
Army of Northern Virginia, 44, 58, 60, 64
Army of Tennessee, 50
Army of the Potomac, 53
artillery, 44
Ashby, Turner, 43

"Beauty," 17–18,
"Bleeding Kansas," 32, 40
Blue Ridge Mountains, 9
Brandy Station, Battle, 63
brigadier general Stuart, 50
Brown, John, 32, **33**, 38–39
Bull Run (see Manassas Junction)

cadets, 17
campaigns, military, 29
captain Stuart, 23
Catlett's Station, 58
cavalry, **26**, 43, 45–46
cavalry officers, 23
Chambersburg, Pennsylvania, 58–59
Chancellorville, Battle of, 42, **56**, 59
Charleston, South Carolina, 40
Cheyenne, 32–34
Civil War, 22, 39
Confederate Army, 40, 60
Confederate soldiers, **48**
Confederate States of America, 22
Cooke, Flora, 30–31
Cooke, Philip St. George, 30, 55
corporal Stuart, 23
Culpeper County, Virginia, 60

Davis, Jefferson, **22**, 29, 69
death of Stuart, 69–70
Don Quixote (Stuart's horse), 23

Early, Jubal, 49
education of Stuart, 11–25
Emory & Henry Methodist college, 12, 14
Ewell, 61

First Cavalry, 29, 32
Fort Kearny, 34
Fort Laramie, 34

Fort Leavenworth, Kansas, 30, 34, 35
Fort McIntosh, Texas, 27
Fort Sumter, 40, **41**
free soilers, 30, 31
free states, 16, 31

G Company, 33
Galveston, Texas, 27
Gettysburg, Pennsylvania, 64–65, **64**

Harpers Ferry, Virginia, 37–39, 40, 43, 44
Hollywood Cemetery, 69–70
Hooker, Joseph, 59, 60

Indian Wars, 28, 32–35, 40
intelligence, 46–49
inventions by Stuart, 36

Jackson, Thomas "Stonewall," 42, 43, 59
Jefferson Barracks, Missouri, 27, 29
Jeffersonian, The, 29
Johnston, Joseph E., 44, 49–50

Kansas territory, 30, 38–40
Kansas–Nebraska Act, 31

Laredo, Texas, 27
Laurel Hill, 8–9
Lee, Custis, 37
Lee, Robert E., 37, **39**, 50, 52–53, 60, 63–65, 71
lightning horse hitcher, 36
Lincoln, Abraham, 40, 53, **54**
Longstreet, James, 54–55, 61

Manassas Junction (Bull Run), first battle of, 44, **45**, 49
Manassas Junction (Bull Run), second battle of, 60, **61**
Manifest Destiny, 16
map of U.S., 1800s, **16**
McClellan, George, 50–53, **54**, 58
Missouri, 27
Mounted Rifles, 27

Native Americans, 26, 28, 32–35, 40
New Orleans, Louisiana, 27

patents by Stuart, 36
Patrick County, Virginia, 7
Piedmont region, 9

77

INDEX

PICTURE CREDITS

page

3: National Archives at College Park
6: Bettmann/Corbis
13: National Archives at College Park
16: Bettmann/Corbis
22: National Archives at College Park
26: HultonArchive by Getty Images
30: National Archives at College Park
33: National Archives at College Park
39: National Archives at College Park
41: National Archives at College Park
42: HultonArchive by Getty Images
45: HultonArchive by Getty Images

48: Bettmann/Corbis
51: HultonArchive by Getty Images
54: HultonArchive by Getty Images
56: Corbis
61: Corbis
64: HultonArchive by Getty Images
67: Corbis

Cover photo: National Archives at College Park

ABOUT THE AUTHOR

MEG GREENE earned a bachelor's degree in history at Lindenwood College in St. Charles, Missouri, and master's degrees from the University of Nebraska at Omaha and the University of Vermont. Ms. Greene is the author of 12 other books, writes regularly for *Cobblestone Magazine* and other publications, and serves as a Contributing Editor for *Suite101.com*'s "History For Children." She makes her home in Virginia, not far from Yellow Tavern and the Stuart Monument.

Northport-East Northport Public Library

JUL 2008

To view your patron record from a computer, click on
the Library's homepage: **www.nenpl.org**

You may:
- request an item be placed on hold
- renew an item that is overdue
- view titles and due dates checked out on your card
- view your own outstanding fines

185 Larkfield Road
East Northport, NY 11731
631-261-2313